101 POEMS
TO KEEP YOU SANE

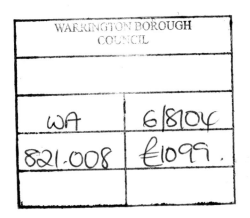

101 POEMS TO KEEP YOU SANE

Emergency Rations
For The Seriously Stressed

EDITED BY

DAISY GOODWIN

with Tabitha Potts

■ HarperCollins*Publishers*

HarperCollins*Publishers*
77–85 Fulham Palace Road,
Hammersmith, London w6 8jb
www.fireandwater.com

Published by HarperCollins*Publishers* 2001
9 8 7 6 5 4 3 2

Full permissions information may be found on pp. 131–34

A catalogue record for this book
is available from the British Library

ISBN 0 00 712796 0

Set in PostScript Linotype Minion with Optima display
Typeset by Rowland Phototypesetting Ltd, Bury St Edmunds, Suffolk

Printed and bound in Great Britain by The Bath Press, Bath

CONTENTS

INTRODUCTION ix

You Have Performed An Illegal
  Action 3
Flatpack Frenzy 7
Too Solid Flesh 9
Domestic Goddess Anxiety 13
Crow's-Feet 18
In Transit 22
You Don't Have To Be Mad To Work
  Here 27
Downsized 33
Endless Winter 35
Hexes For Your Ex 37
Low Blood Sugar 40
Can't Sleep 43
Mental Massage 46
Only Connect 50
50 Ways To Leave Your Lover 54
Baby Love 58
Through Thick and Thin 62
Enough Already 66

How To Be A Perfect Parent 69
L Plates 72
Time To Grow Up 76
Wanting A Child 79
Do The Right Thing 83
Other People's Money 88
Unholy Matrimony 92
Why Are They Looking At Me Like
  That? 96
Be Here Now 99
Getting Over It 104
Saying Goodbye 111
Black Hole 117
Emotional Rescue 121
What Are You Waiting For? 125

ACKNOWLEDGEMENTS 131
INDEX OF POETS 135
INDEX 139

In memory of Esmé Lara Harman

UPON A CHILD

Here a pretty baby lies,
Sung asleep with lullabies.
Pray be silent and not stir
The easy earth that covers her.

Robert Herrick

INTRODUCTION

Modern life continually nibbles away at your sanity. How can you keep your head while all around are losing theirs, in a world that includes two-minute answermachine messages, Ikea, wayward supermarket trolleys, train delays, Powerpoint presentations, and white vans? Minor irritations perhaps, but their cumulative effect is like your overdraft: you do nothing to encourage it but the wretched thing never really goes away. The sad truth is that the only sure way to banish life's minor miseries, the leaves rustling at the bottom of the Beaufort scale, is to have real disaster strike, the Force Ten gale of bereavement or heartbreak. These are the moments you look back on your pre-tragedy life and wonder why you didn't bother to be happy when you had the chance.

So don't wait for catastrophe to give you back your sense of priorities. Let the poems in this book help you put your life in proportion. Every time I read the Michael Longley poem 'Out There' that goes: 'Do they ever meet out there/ The dolphins I counted/ The otter I wait for?/ I should have spent my life/ Listening to the waves,' I can feel my mind shifting focus; life's immediate irritations blur and the things that matter come sharply into focus on the horizon.

There are other ways, of course, to transcend the minor frictions of modern life: you could pay people to teach you to walk over hot stones, you could fire paintballs at the accounts department on a Friday afternoon in Surrey, you could buy an olive grove in Tuscany, you could even have an affair. But the poems in this book are a much quicker, cheaper and easier route to sorting your head out. The process of reading a poem, trying to tease out the meaning from the clotted tangle of words, concentrates the mind – you can't pay full attention to a poem and worry about where you put your dry-cleaning stubs. Reciting the words in your head (anything more public is definitely stressful), lets their rhythm and order smooth the worry grooves in your mind. And above all, really listen to what the poems have to say; these two lines from Wordsworth contain pretty much everything you need to know about what's wrong with modern life: 'The world is too much with us, late and soon/ Getting and spending, we lay waste our powers.'

This book is organised in ascending order of turmoil. It starts with things that merely ruffle the otherwise calm surface of life: wayward technology, dodgy DIY, love handles, non-existent trains. Further in there are sections to help you weather life's prevailing winds, the north-easterly chill of losing your job, or reaching a milestone birthday in the Downsized and Crow's-Feet sections, as well as the balmy but no less powerful southerly breezes of having a baby, falling in love, and raising your children in Baby Love, L Plates and How To Be a Perfect Parent.

The last third of the book is your defence against the violent storms and hurricanes of bereavement, heartbreak, infertility and depression: the poems here can't take away the pain but they are at least testimony to the universality of suffering. I think the Auden poem 'Musée des Beaux Arts' is the most lucid retort to the unanswerable cry of 'Why Me?'

Some of the poems, such as those in the Emotional Rescue section, are for emergencies only; read them all the time and they will lose their punch. Others are worth reading every day: turn to Mental Massage and Be Here Now on a regular basis and build up your immunity to modern madness. When things become unbearable at the office I always make a point of reading the Richard LeGallienne poem that starts 'I meant to do my work today . . .' How many days spent virtuously earning a living do we actually remember as opposed to the memorable days spent doing nothing much? And I recommend the E. E. Cummings poem that begins, 'in time's a noble mercy of proportion', when you think you can't resolve the conflict between work and life. Not that this book advocates irresponsible hedonism . . .

The last section is called What Are You Waiting For? and is a reminder, if you needed one, that each day we get closer to what W. E. Henley terms 'the ruffian on the stair'. So if you don't like your body, your job, your marriage, then do something about it. As Omar Khayyam famously wrote:

> The moving finger writes, and having writ,
> Moves on: nor all thy Piety nor wit
> Shall lure it back to cancel half a Line
> Nor all thy Tears wash out a Word of it.

Scary stuff, but liberating too.

Finally I would like to thank all those who collaborated in compiling this anthology: the readers of my previous books who wrote or emailed me with suggestions; Joanna Coles for remembering Norman Cameron's brilliant poem 'The Compassionate Fool'; Nicola from the bookshop in Bridport for some great poems and for lending me her books; Rashna Nekoo and Kristie Morris for their support and patience and my daughter Ottilie for scouring books and the internet for suitable poems. I am also very grateful to Mary Enright and all her fabulously knowledgeable staff at the Poetry Library in the South Bank Centre for letting me pick their brains and use their photocopier, and to Connie Hallam for tackling the near impossible task of copyright clearances. Special thanks go to my sister Tabitha who has helped me compile this book at a time when her life was unimaginably bleak. Poetry can be a great healer.

101 POEMS
TO KEEP YOU SANE

YOU HAVE PERFORMED AN ILLEGAL ACTION

Gadgets have an insidious way of undermining your sanity. They work perfectly at first, purring into life at the press of a button and effortlessly working out your VAT, telling you the time in Ecuador, showing the quickest route from Droitwich to Crewe. But then, maybe you don't show them enough respect; perhaps you forget to show them proudly to your friends, you stop fondling them on the tube, in short you take them for granted. And it's at that moment that your digital darling takes its revenge by crashing in the middle of the document you have to finish by lunchtime, or your phone develops an underwater crackle when you are trying to get directions for a meeting you are already twenty minutes late for, or the mildly obscene text message you intended for your lover lights up your spouse's LED instead. Preserve your peace of mind. Don't put your trust in anything that needs an AA battery.

Pls, stop sendg msgs2ths
no, i am not linda,
I hv not slept w/yr sis,
+i wd nvr call any1's ma a slag.
Gd luk w/viag.
Luv, yr wrong no. xxx

Charlotte Fortune

Spellbound

I have a spell in chequer
It came with my pea see.
It plane Leigh Marx four my revue
Miss takes eye ken knot sea.
I've run this poem threw IT
I'm shore your plea zed too no;
Its let a perfect in it's weigh
My check her tolled me sew.

Norman Vandal

Modern Times

I have never signed
the peace pact with machinery
never can open car doors
or even a can for that matter.

I peck my way through typewriters
smudging and swearing like a coal miner
and always wind up with tape recorders
like an Englishman eating spaghetti.

The Indians signed it
and see what happened to them
herded by tractors onto reservations:
the immigrants signed it

and were stuffed into canneries
to baby-sit conveyor belts.
The President has signed it
even the Pope has signed it

but I will never sign
the peace pact with machinery
I will fight it tooth and throttle.
Every car that turns up my drive

is always carried off on a stretcher.
My record players become deaf mutes
my glare makes TVs catatonic and
vacuum cleaners bite the dust.

I live in a quiet rain forest
with no car and much license
where even the egg beater
is not my best friend.

James Nolan

FLATPACK FRENZY

It all looked so simple. You needed a chest of drawers/TV stand/wardrobe and there it was in the shop: clearly designed, competitively priced and they had it in stock. Somehow you didn't imagine that all that sleekly contoured blond wood and storage potential would emerge in a long flat cardboard box impossible to fit in the boot of any vehicle other than a hearse. And then, at home, your fingers lacerated by the maliciously placed bronze staples, your sitting room carpet swamped by moulting pieces of MDF, you smooth out the crumpled assembly instructions only to find that they refer to a Scandinavian parallel universe where all screws are the right length and corners are always 90 degrees. Neither of these poems explains why Slot A won't line up with Slot B, but the first might conjure a smile and 'Upon the Snail' by John Bunyan is a hint about the qualities you will need to finish the job.

Screw It Yourself

With each turn it do make within its Hole
A Screw should advance towards its Goal.
If it fails in this Task, let the Blame fall
On the Screw, the Screw-Driver or the Wall.

Adrian Mitchell

Upon the Snail

She goes but softly, but she goeth sure;
   She stumbles not as stronger creatures do:
Her journey's shorter, so she may endure
   Better than they which do much further go.

She makes no noise, but stilly seizeth on
   The flower or herb appointed for her food,
The which she quietly doth feed upon,
   While others range, and gare, but find no good.

And though she doth but very softly go,
   However 'tis not fast, nor slow, but sure;
And certainly they that do travel so,
   The prize they do aim at they do procure.

John Bunyan

TOO SOLID FLESH

Having recently had a baby, I wake up every morning full of mirror-induced resolve – today is the day I am going to rediscover my waist and give up dairy, wheat, chocolate in favour of spring water and celery. On a good day I can last till 2.30 before my body becomes less of a temple to pure living and more of a shrine to Cadbury's Heroes. The Alice Walker poem will have you lifting those weights but the Wendy Cope poem will make you feel less guilty about the double *frappuccino* with extra cream that you just had to have afterwards. Following Hilaire Belloc's dietary advice avoids the ritual humiliation of Weight Watchers, and is probably just as effective.

Every Morning

Every morning I exercise
my body.
It complains
'Why are you doing this to me?'
I give it a plié
in response.
I heave my legs
off the floor
and feel my stomach muscles
rebel:
they are mutinous
there are rumblings
of dissent.

I have other things
to show,
but mostly, my body.
'Don't you see that person
staring at you?' I ask my breasts,
which are still capable
of staring back.
'If I didn't exercise
you couldn't look up
that far.
Your life would be nothing
but shoes.'
'Let us at least say we're doing it
for ourselves';
my fingers are eloquent;
they never sweat.

Alice Walker

The New Regime

Yes, I agree. We'll pull ourselves together.
We eat too much. We're always getting pissed.
It's not a bad idea to find out whether
We like each other sober. Let's resist.
I've got the Perrier and the carrot-grater,
I'll look on a Scotch or a pudding as a crime.
We all have to be sensible sooner or later
But don't let's be sensible all the time.

No more thinking about a second bottle
And saying 'What the hell?' and giving in.
Tomorrow I'll be jogging at full throttle
To make myself successful, rich and thin.
A healthy life's a great rejuvenator
But, God, it's going to be an uphill climb.
We all have to be sensible sooner or later
But don't let's be sensible all the time.

The conversation won't be half as trivial –
You'll hold forth on the issues of the day –
And, when our evenings aren't quite so convivial,
You'll start remembering the things I say.
Oh, see if you can catch the eye of the waiter
And order me a double vodka and lime.
We all have to be sensible sooner or later
But I refuse to be sensible all the time.

Wendy Cope

The Vulture

The Vulture eats between his meals
   And that's the reason why
He very, very rarely feels
   As well as you and I.

His eye is dull, his head is bald,
   His neck is growing thinner.
Oh! what a lesson for us all
   To only eat at dinner!

Hilaire Belloc

DOMESTIC GODDESS ANXIETY

When I was growing up women discovered that being houseproud was a
waste of time. Out went sheets and blankets and in came duvets, easy care
polyester and Shirley Conran's famous phrase about life being too short to
stuff a mushroom. These days, as if we haven't got enough to worry about,
any reader of the glossy magazines will be made to feel if not exactly
guilty, then certainly inadequate, if we don't bake our own digestive
biscuits in our pristine kitchens full of lavender-scented laundry and
creatively playing children. I'm all for celebrating simple pleasures as the
American poet Marge Piercy does in her poem 'Folding Sheets', but these
tasks are only truly enjoyable if there is some element of choice involved.
Most domestic routine is simply drudgery. I include Wendy Cope's poem
'The Sorrow of Socks' for anyone who loads the washing machine; you
are not alone in possessing a Bermuda Triangle for hosiery.

Folding Sheets

They must be clean.
There ought to be two of you
to talk as you work, your
eyes and hands meeting.
They can be crisp, a little rough
and fragrant from the line;
or hot from the dryer
as from an oven. A silver
grey kitten with amber
eyes to dart among
the sheets and wrestle and leap out
helps. But mostly pleasure
lies in the clean linen
slapping into shape.

Whenever I fold a fitted sheet
making the moves that are like
closing doors, I feel my mother.
The smell of clean laundry is hers.

Marge Piercy

On a Tired Housewife

Here lies a poor woman who was always tired,
She lived in a house where help wasn't hired:
Her last words on earth were: 'Dear friends, I am going
To where there's no cooking, or washing, or sewing,
For everything there is exact to my wishes,
For where they don't eat there's no washing of dishes.
I'll be where loud anthems will always be ringing,
But having no voice I'll be quit of the singing.
Don't mourn for me now, don't mourn for me never,
I am going to do nothing for ever and ever.'

Anon.

Twelve Things I Don't Want to Hear

Assemble this in eight straightforward steps.
Start with a fish stock, made the day before.
The driver has arrived but, sadly, drunk.
We'll need some disinfectant for the floor.

Ensure all surfaces are clean and dry.
There's been a problem, Madam, I'm afraid!
We'd better have the manhole cover up.
Apologies, the doctor's been delayed.

I'd love to bring a friend, he's so depressed.
They've put you on the camp bed in the hall.
There's just one table left, perhaps you'd share?
I know it's midnight, but I had to call . . .

Connie Bensley

The Sorrow of Socks

Some socks are loners –
They can't live in pairs.
On washdays they've shown us
They want to be loners.
They puzzle their owners,
They hide in dark lairs.
Some socks are loners –
They won't live in pairs.

Wendy Cope

CROW'S-FEET

These poems are for the day when you get your holiday snaps back and you are faced with undeniable evidence that you should have listened to the song and used sunscreen. But take heart, demographics are on your side: forty is the new thirty and pretty soon we will all be thinking of ourselves as vintages maturing magnificently, positively looking forward to what D. H. Lawrence calls 'wrinkled ripe fulfilment'. And if not, there are an awful lot of plastic surgeons in Brazil.

Crossing the Border

Senescence begins
And middle age ends
The day your descendants
Outnumber your friends

Ogden Nash

On Reaching Forty

Other acquainted years
sidle
with modest
decorum
across the scrim of toughened
tears and to a stage
planked with laughter boards
and waxed with rueful loss
But forty
with the authorized
brazenness of a uniformed
cop stomps
no-knocking
into the script
bumps a funky grind on the
shabby curtain of youth
and delays the action.

Unless you have the inborn
wisdom
and grace
and are clever enough
to die at
thirty-nine.

Maya Angelou

Getting Older

The first surprise: I like it.
Whatever happens now, some things
that used to terrify have not:

I didn't die young, for instance. Or lose
my only love. My three children
never had to run away from anyone.

Don't tell me this gratitude is complacent.
We all approach the edge of the same blackness
which for me is silent.

Knowing as much sharpens
my delight in January freesia,
hot coffee, winter sunlight. So we say

as we lie close on some gentle occasion:
every day won from such
darkness is a celebration.

Elaine Feinstein

Beautiful Old Age

It ought to be lovely to be old
to be full of the peace that comes of experience
and wrinkled ripe fulfilment.

The wrinkled smile of completeness that follows a life
lived undaunted and unsoured with accepted lies.
If people lived without accepting lies
they would ripen like apples, and be scented like pippins
in their old age.

Soothing, old people should be, like apples
when one is tired of love.
Fragrant like yellowing leaves, and dim with the soft
stillness and satisfaction of autumn.

And a girl should say:
It must be wonderful to live and grow old.
Look at my mother, how rich and still she is! –

And a young man should think: By Jove
my father has faced all weathers, but it's been a life! –

D. H. Lawrence

IN TRANSIT

Grim journeys you make every day: to work, to school, wherever – your mind on autopilot, your life on hold until you get there – then the train stops, the red lights ahead of you cluster like malign strawberries, voices impart vital information intelligible only to the listeners in Jodrell Bank, and you are suspended in a bubble of metal waiting for the world to start again. The well prepared traveller will have a slim volume to hand; poetry is wonderful for those moments of silent captivity and so much kinder to the other passengers than the thump and boom of the Walkman. I suppose that very soon the stranded traveller will be able to download suitably consoling poems from cyberspace. That's the theory anyway, for the practice see the poems under the You Have Performed An Illegal Action section. (And I make no apologies to the current rail operators for including a poem called 'British Rail Regrets' – sadly nothing about this poem seems out of date.)

Here's an announcement. Quite soon, platform eight
Will shortly be leaving a few minutes late.
Would cynics on board please not draw the conclusion
The train is in motion. This simple illusion
Will soon be dispelled when at quarter to three,
Their friends on the platform reach Devon for tea.

Alan Ayckbourn

British Rail Regrets

British Rail regrets
having to regret.
British Rail regrets
it cannot spell.
British Rail regrets
the chalk ran out.
British Rail regrets
that due to a staff shortage
there will be no one
to offer regrets.
British Rail regrets
but will not be sending
flowers or tributes.
British Rail regrets
the early arrival
of your train.
This was due to industrious action.
British Rail regrets
that because of a work-to-rule
by our tape machine
this is a real person.
British Rail regrets
the cheese shortage
in your sandwich.
This is due to
a points failure.
The steward got
three out of ten.

British Rail regrets.
Tears flow from beneath
the locked doors of the staff rooms.
red-eyed ticket collectors
offer comfort
to stranded passengers.
Angry drivers threaten
to come out in sympathy
with the public.
British Rail regrets.
That's why its members
are permanently dressed in black.
That's why porters stand around
as if in a state of shock.
That's why Passenger Information
is off the hook. British Rail regrets
that due to the shortage of regrets
there will be a train.

Steve Turner

The Highway

It seems too enormous just for a man to be
Walking on. As if it and the empty day
Were all there is. And a little dog
Trotting in time with the heat waves, off
Near the horizon, seeming never to get
Any farther. The sun and everything
Are stuck in the same places, and the ditch
Is the same all the time, full of every kind
Of bone, while the empty air keeps humming
That sound it has memorized of things going
Past. And the signs with huge heads and starved
Bodies, doing dances in the heat,
And the others big as houses, all promise
But with nothing inside and only one wall,
Tell of other places where you can eat,
Drink, get a bath, lie on a bed
Listening to music, and be safe. If you
Look around you see it is just the same
The other way, going back; and farther
Now to where you came from, probably,
Than to places you can reach by going on.

W. S. Merwin

Journeys

The deception of platforms
where the arrivals and the departures
coincide. And the smiles
on the faces of those welcoming

and bidding farewell are
to conceal the knowledge
that destinations are the familiarities
from which the traveller must set out.

R. S. Thomas

YOU DON'T HAVE TO BE MAD TO WORK HERE

Anthropologists of the next millennium will earn their doctorates writing papers about 'The Coffee Break: the role of stimulants in early twenty-first century office rituals'. Museums of the future will vie with each other to acquire a perfectly preserved devotional drinking vessel inscribed with the sacred text, 'You don't have to be mad to work here, but it helps'. Children of the future will go on school trips to model offices where they will dress up as bosses and secretaries and re-enact the rite of the photocopier. If your office occasionally seems as foreign to you as an ancient civilisation then read these poems in your lunchbreak – much better for your blood pressure than a skinny *latte* to go.

The Meeting

In the long and boring meeting,
in the hot and boring meeting,
there was shouting by the Chairman,
bullying almost by the Chairman,
people rose on points of order,
caused chaos with points of order,
argument became emotive,
all the words used were emotive,
and this was the obvious reason
passion overcame all reason.

Everything was twice repeated,
sometimes more than twice repeated,
as they worked through the agenda
(it seemed elastic, that agenda,
becoming longer, never shorter),
their utterances grew long, not shorter,

it was just like spreading butter,
words went further, like spread butter,
covering each subject thinly,
covering almost nothing thinly.

People talked about resigning,
disgruntled talk was of resigning,
accusations in a covey
flew like partridge in a covey,
yet this was not entertaining –
it sounds like drama, entertaining
as the TV scenes in courtrooms –
this was *not* like scenes in courtrooms,
it contrived to be quite boring,
really quite immensely boring.

It was more like scenes where children
shout insults at other children,
it was like a verbal punch-up,
more long-winded than a punch-up,
but the bitterness and anger
brought out words like knives in anger,
it was more like verbal murder
if there's boredom in a murder –
any moderate survivors
in the end *felt* like survivors.

Like being rescued from a snowstorm,
or blinding words whirled like a snowstorm;
they could only cry for brandy,
go to pubs and order brandy,

they felt they deserved some medals
like the Army's campaign medals –
through the tumult and the shouting
(quiet was strange after the shouting)
they achieved the peace of something
through the meeting – which was something.

It was like peace after beating
heads on walls, like hours of beating
heads on walls and never stopping –
till at last the joy of stopping
seemed a truly great achievement,
lack of pain, a great achievement,
it's so lovely when you stop it!
Negative delight, to stop it,
flooded through them after meeting
at that long hot boring meeting!

Gavin Ewart

Then the Time Comes

Then the time comes when you know
none of your promise will be fulfilled;
the saving roles luck, fame, deliverance
from your job were meant to play . . .
You will slave on till pension day,
eluded by advancement, satisfaction, wealth.
In your head, some plangent melody repeats;
in your mind's eye, a preview of your part
as walk-on stoic, accepting failure in good
heart, battling home against the wind
this night the same as the last.

Dennis O'Driscoll

Office Party

I think I enjoyed the party.
I cannot remember it well.
My stomach is churning in circles
and my poor head is hurting like hell.

I think I enjoyed the buffet,
but the crab paste was long past its best.
The quiche was awash with heaven knows what
and the salad was limp and depressed.

The cheese cubes on sticks were all crusted,
the vol-au-vents soggy and stale,
the trifle was dusted with fag ash
and smelt less of sherry than ale.

I think I enjoyed the fruit cup,
and a glass of the manager's wine.
The gin and the Scotch and the vodka
all left me feeling just fine.

The problems began with the brandy –
one sip of it went to my head.
I remember removing my stockings,
and then . . . oh, I wish I was dead.

I seem to remember the records,
they played all my favourite sounds.
I started the conga to 'Nights in White Satin'
and cha-cha'd to 'Send in the Clowns.'

Then somebody danced on the table
and sat on the manager's knee,
and did something crude with the manager's hat,
and – oh glory, I think it was me.

My memory's starting to focus.
I remember the manager's face
when I told him I hated the work and the staff
and just what he could do with the place.

I think I enjoyed the party –
one over the eight is no crime,
but reviewing last night in the cold light of day,
I think I had better resign.

Alison Chisholm

DOWNSIZED

Losing your job is never easy. Don't believe them when they say this is as hard for me as it is for you, because it isn't. Once they've done the dirty deed, they can move on, you are the one who is unemployed. That said, I've only been fired once in my life and it was the best thing that ever happened to me, so look on your P45 as a liberation not a sentence. I think 'The Compassionate Fool' by Norman Cameron is the only smart way to think about the person who 'lets you go'. But if you're looking for something stronger try the Hexes For Your Ex section.

Redundancy Pay

Redundancy pay
Is not a bad way
To learn at last
You're a thing of the past.

Reay Fuller

The Compassionate Fool

My enemy had bidden me as guest.
His table all set out with wine and cake,
His ordered chairs, he to beguile me dressed
So neatly, moved my pity for his sake.

I knew it was an ambush, but could not
Leave him to eat his cake up by himself
And put his unused glasses on the shelf.
I made pretence of falling in his plot,

And trembled when in his anxiety
He bared it too absurdly to my view.
And even as he stabbed me through and through
I pitied him for his small strategy.

Norman Cameron

ENDLESS WINTER

The grey afternoon that seems to stretch from the end of October to June makes that permafrost layer of smiling optimism necessary to withstand modern madness, even harder to maintain. These poems won't make the sun come out, but they might make you smile . . .

A Stone

A stone at its core,
this snowball's the porcelain
knob on winter's door.

Paul Muldoon

No!

No sun – no moon!
No morn – no noon –
No dawn – no dusk – no proper time of day –
No sky – no earthly view –
No distance looking blue –
No road – no street – no 't'other side the way' –
No end to any Row –
No indications where the Crescents go –
No top to any steeple –
No recognitions of familiar people –
No courtesies for showing 'em –
No knowing 'em! –
No travelling at all – no locomotion,
No inkling of the way – no notion –
No go; – by land or ocean –
No mail – no post –
No news from any foreign coast –
No Park – no Ring – no afternoon gentility –
No company – no nobility –
No warmth, no cheerfulness, no healthful ease,
No comfortable feel in any member –
No shade, no shine, no butterflies, no bees,
No fruits, no flowers, no leaves, no birds –
November!

Thomas Hood

HEXES FOR YOUR EX

A selection of really savage poems for those days when closure is hard to come by and you've run out of places to put the pin in the voodoo doll. The Australian poet Vicki Raymond provides a marvellously comprehensive curse, and James Fenton's poem is perfect for anyone who left too much unsaid. But remember, these poems are for very, very bad days, when you receive an invitation to your ex's wedding for example. If you are resorting to hexes on a regular basis, I suggest you turn to the Getting Over It section and move on.

The Sending of Five

Five potent curses
I send you, the first
love, which frequently
drives men to suffer
uncouth hair transplants.

The second, riches,
bringing in their train
the envy of friends
expressed in these words:
'It's alright for some.'

My third curse is fame:
may you become sport
for reporters, may
the dull quote you, may
cranks think they *are* you.

My fourth, contentment,
hugging you, white grub,
in a fat cocoon
that the cries of men
cannot penetrate.

And last, a longlife.
May you live to be
called 'The Grand Old Man.'
Smiling at you, may
the young sprain their jaws.

Vicki Raymond

Let's Go Over It All Again

Some people are like that.
They split up and then they think:
Hey, maybe we haven't hurt each other to the uttermost.
Let's meet up and have a drink.

Let's go over it all again.
Let's rake over the dirt.
Let me pick that scab of yours.
Does it hurt?

Let's go over what went wrong –
How and why and when.
Let's go over what went wrong
Again and again.

We hurt each other badly once.
We said a lot of nasty stuff.
But lately I've been thinking how
I didn't hurt you enough.

Maybe there's more where that came from,
Something more malign.
Let me damage you again
For the sake of auld lang syne.

Yes, let me see you bleed again
For the sake of auld lang syne.

James Fenton

LOW BLOOD SUGAR

There are days when sushi just won't cut it anymore and BSE and high lipid levels notwithstanding all you want is a nice juicy steak and chips with chocolate chip ice cream to follow. Maya Angelou has written a poem to fortify you in your quest for saturated fat. I also include a handy recipe for the perfect salad just in case you need to refresh your palate.

The Health-Food Diner

No sprouted wheat and soya shoots
And Brussels in a cake,
Carrot straw and spinach raw,
(Today, I need a steak).

Not thick brown rice and rice pilau
Or mushrooms creamed on toast,
Turnips mashed and parsnips hashed,
(I'm dreaming of a roast).

Health-food folks around the world
Are thinned by anxious zeal,
They look for help in seafood kelp
(I count on breaded veal).

No Smoking signs, raw mustard greens,
Zucchini by the ton,
Uncooked kale and bodies frail
Are sure to make me run

to

Loins of pork and chicken thighs
And standing rib, so prime,
Pork chops brown and fresh ground round
(I crave them all the time).

Irish stews and boiled corned beef
and hot dogs by the scores,
or any place that saves a space
For smoking carnivores.

Maya Angelou

Recipe for a Salad

To make this condiment, your poet begs
The pounded yellow of two hard-boiled eggs;
Two boiled potatoes, passed through kitchen-sieve,
Smoothness and softness to the salad give;
Let onion atoms lurk within the bowl,
And, half-suspected, animate the whole.
Of mordant mustard add a single spoon,
Distrust the condiment that bites so soon;
But deem it not, thou man of herbs, a fault,
To add a double quantity of salt,
And, lastly, o'er the flavored compound toss
A magic soup-spoon of anchovy sauce.
Oh, green and glorious! Oh, herbaceous treat!
'T would tempt the dying anchorite to eat;
Back to the world he'd turn his fleeting soul,
And plunge his fingers in the salad bowl!
Serenely full, the epicure would say,
Fate can not harm me, I have dined to-day!

Sydney Smith

CAN'T SLEEP

My own remedy to insomnia is a novel by Anthony Trollope. His stories of cathedral close intrigue and wayward heiresses are entertaining enough to keep troubling thoughts out of your head but not so gripping that they will keep you awake. But if Victorian novelists don't work for you, the doctor won't give you any more Temazepam and you can't stomach any more Horlicks, then there's nothing for it but to follow one of the more useful bits of advice found in a poem, 'Just heave yourself out, make the tea, and give in.'

Here we are all, by day; by night we're hurled
By dreams, each one, into a several world.

Robert Herrick

Insomnia

It's like waiting for someone to leave –
someone tedious, garrulous
and worryingly manic.
Someone full of reminiscences
which you don't want to hear about.

It's like waiting for something
to be taken away – something
with a buzz as maddening as tinnitus;
something you've grown tired of, which is
taking up space.

These things multiply, creak and throw shadows
round the room. They start asking
upsetting questions.
Lie doggo. This is not
an interrogation chamber.

The clock strikes again.
To pass the time,
you could try making up anagrams.
You could start with
ABSENCE and OBLIVION.

Connie Bensley

6 a.m. Thoughts

As soon as you wake they come blundering in
   Like puppies or importunate children;
What was a landscape emerging from mist
   Becomes at once a disordered garden.

And the mess they trail with them! Embarrassments,
   Anger, lust fear – in fact the whole pig-pen;
And who'll clean it up? No hope for sleep now –
   Just heave yourself out, make the tea, and give in.

Dick Davis

MENTAL MASSAGE

These are the poems you need after one of the nights described in the previous section when the world seems a particularly unfriendly place. Before you snap at the milkman for daring to present his bill for the third week running or scowl at the unfortunate old lady who took your seat on the bus, read Sheenagh Pugh's poem 'Sometimes'. Days, like investments, can go up as well as down.

An Epilogue

I have seen flowers come in stony places
And kind things done by men with ugly faces,
And the gold cup won by the worst horse at the races,
So I trust, too.

John Masefield

Sometimes

Sometimes things don't go, after all,
from bad to worse. Some years, muscadel
faces down frost; green thrives; the crops don't fail,
sometimes a man aims high, and all goes well.

A people sometimes will step back from war;
elect an honest man; decide they care
enough, that they can't leave some stranger poor.
Some men become what they were born for.

Sometimes our best efforts do not go
amiss; sometimes we do as we meant to.
The sun will sometimes melt a field of sorrow
that seemed hard frozen: may it happen for you.

Sheenagh Pugh

Give Yourself a Hug

Give yourself a hug
when you feel unloved

Give yourself a hug
when people put on airs
to make you feel a bug

Give yourself a hug
when everyone seems to give you
a cold-shoulder shrug

Give yourself a hug—
a big big hug

And keep on singing,
'Only one in a million like me
Only one in a million-billion-thrillion-zillion
like me.'

Grace Nichols

New Every Morning

Every day is a fresh beginning,
Listen my soul to the glad refrain.
   And, spite of old sorrows
      And older sinning,
      Troubles forecasted
      And possible pain,
Take heart with the day and begin again.

Susan Coolidge

ONLY CONNECT

The definition of the power balance in a relationship used to be between the one who kissed and the one who offered their cheek. The modern definition of love should make the distinction between the lover who telephones and the one who waits for their call. It is, sadly, one of life's unbreakable rules that a watched telephone never rings.

Lots of Things

Lots of things
can be laughable
such as
kissing my phone
when I have heard
your voice in it.

Not to kiss my phone
when I cannot kiss you
would be
still more laughable
and sadder

Erich Fried

Message

Pick up the phone before it is too late
And dial my number. There's no time to spare –
Love is already turning into hate
And very soon I'll start to look elsewhere.

Good, old-fashioned men like you are rare –
You want to get to know me at a rate
That's guaranteed to drive me to despair.
Pick up the phone before it is too late.

Well, wouldn't it be nice to consummate
Our friendship while we've still got teeth and hair?
Just bear in mind that you are forty-eight
And dial my number. There's no time to spare.

Another kamikaze love affair?
No chance. This time I'll have to learn to wait
But one more day is more than I can bear –
Love is already turning into hate.

Of course, my friends say I exaggerate
And dramatize a lot. That may be fair
But it is no fun being in this state
And very soon I'll start to look elsewhere.

I know you like me but I wouldn't dare
Ring you again. Instead I'll concentrate
On sending thought-waves through the London air
And, if they reach you, please don't hesitate –
Pick up the phone.

Wendy Cope

The Telephone

It comes in black
and blue, indecisive
beige. In red and chaperons my life.
Sitting like a strict
and spinstered Aunt spiked between my needs
and need.

It tats the day, crocheting
other people's lives
in neat arrangements
ignoring me
busy with the hemming
of strangers' overlong affairs or
the darning of my
neighbors' worn-out
dreams.

From Monday, the morning of the week,
through mid-times
noon and Sunday's dying
light. It sits silent.
Its needle sound
does not transfix my ear
or draw my longing to
a close.

Ring. Damn you!

Maya Angelou

50 WAYS TO LEAVE YOUR LOVER

There are countless poems about being left (see the Getting Over It section), but I thought it only fair to include some words of advice for the leavers. The Stevie Smith poem is wonderfully ruthless, even the most deluded suitor can't misinterpret 'I would always very much rather, dear, Live in a tent.' I include the Henry Normal and the Robert Frost poems as a warning to the leaver not to use the phrase, 'But we'll still be friends.'

Lady 'Rogue' Singleton

Come, wed me, Lady Singleton,
And we will have a baby soon
And we will live in Edmonton
Where all the friendly people run.

I could never make you happy darling,
Or give you the baby you want,
I would always very much rather, dear,
Live in a tent.

I am not a cold woman, Henry,
But I do not feel for you,
What I feel for the elephants and the miasmas
And the general view.

Stevie Smith

Ten Ways to End a Relationship

(after Adrian Mitchell)

1. PATRIOTIC
I've got to dedicate myself to work of national importance.

2. SNOBBISH
Your time allocation has expired.

3. OVERWEENING
You are too fine a human to be held back by constraints.

4. PIOUS
I shall pray you find happiness elsewhere.

5. MELODRAMATIC
I'll kill myself rather than go through this torture any
    longer.

6. PATHETIC
I'm not worthy of love. I can't stand anyone to see me like
    this.

7. DEFENSIVE
I don't have to give any reasons.

8. SINISTER
I've been sleepwalking with a bread-knife lately.

9. LECHEROUS
I want to fuck your best friend.

10. PHILOSOPHICAL
Well were we really going out anyway?

Henry Normal

Fire and Ice

Some say the world will end in fire,
Some say in ice.
From what I've tasted of desire
I hold with those who favor fire.
But if it had to perish twice,
I think I know enough of hate
To say that for destruction ice
Is also great
And would suffice.

Robert Frost

BABY LOVE

Nothing prepares you for this, that your new baby goes to the back of your heart and discovers a whole new continent of love. The first few weeks *postpartum* are a time of epiphany for many women: that heady combination of weariness, responsibility and all consuming love combine to make the outside world seem new and strange. Sylvia Plath's poem comes closest to describing that altered state. Sally Emerson's poem 'Back to Work' will be painfully familiar to anybody who has just gone through that rite of passage. I also include a poem called 'All Tears' by my sister which she wrote after the death of her two-day-old daughter because not only is it a beautiful poem but it is a reminder that a healthy baby is a blessing not a right.

Sun, Moon, Stars

Sun, moon, stars,
You that move in the heavens,
Hear this mother!
A new life has come among you.
Make its life smooth.

Virginia Driving Hawk Sneve

Child

Your clear eye is the one absolutely beautiful thing.
I want to fill it with colour and ducks,
The zoo of the new

Whose names you meditate –
April snowdrop, Indian pipe,
Little

Stalk without wrinkle,
Pool in which images
Should be grand and classical

Not this troublous
Wringing of hands, this dark
Ceiling without a star.

Sylvia Plath

Back to Work

The world enters my body,
Runs its vast red buses
Through my stomach,
Swerves into my heart
Causing havoc.
Inside, telephones ring,
Typewriters ram their
Sharp metal keys into my mind.
There is dust on the windows, on the
Desks, on the piling paperwork.
Even the sunshine here is
Made of grey
And nothing is as it should be.

Meanwhile, my darling girl
Sleeps and smiles and laughs, her face
So full of curiosity and magic
That I know the world was
Made in her honour.
She looks around her and as she looks
She renews all she sees.
The leaves rustle excitedly,
The curtains dance by the window,
The shadow moves beside her as
She turns and she turns and she turns,
Ocean eyes,
Taking it all in.

Sally Emerson

All Tears

I'm weeping tears of milk and blood and water
Sculpting my flesh into a new shape: a weeping woman
Transfixed by grief: no one can take this cup from me
O daughter, your death is my Gethsemane

Your fluttering life beat in me like a bird
Caged in flesh. You burst out in a rush of blood
And flew away too soon. Too soon I loved
And lost you to time, my precious dove

Your petal soft skin, cat-eyes open to the light
Now closed, your soft cry, a breath I heard in the night
By my ear: now you are gone, all now lie
In endless sleep. Why did you have to die?

There is no answer. Now the chain of days
Hangs round my neck like millstones
Bowing my head. How can you not hear? Listen
Your mother weeps; your father is silent.

Tabitha Potts

THROUGH THICK AND THIN

Friendships are like houseplants, they need constant attention, regular feeding and watering and they have a nasty habit of shrivelling up for no reason. But a real friend, the thousandth man or woman that Kipling talks about, is made of sterner stuff, a sturdy aspidistra among moody African violets. If you have one look after them; a friend is the best defence against modern madness.

To Someone Who Insisted I Look Up Someone

I rang them up while touring Timbuctoo,
Those bosom chums to whom you're known as '*Who?*'

X. J. Kennedy

A Snarl for Loose Friends

Many who say friend,
friend, clutch their balls like prayers
for fear something of themselves
may break loose and get away.

Many who mumble love,
love keep an eye fixed for the fire
ladder, the exit hatch and at the first
sign of trouble do not hang around to chat.

Many who talk of community
called the real estate agent last night
and the papers are drawn up to sell their land
to a nuclear power plant that shows dirty movies.

Don't count your friends by their buttons
until you have seen them pushed a few times.

Marge Piercy

The Thousandth Man

One man in a thousand, Solomon says,
Will stick more close than a brother.
And it's worth while seeking him half your days
If you find him before the other.
Nine hundred and ninety-nine depend
On what the world sees in you,
But the Thousandth Man will stand your friend
With the whole round world agin you.

'Tis neither promise nor prayer nor show
Will settle the finding for 'ee.
Nine hundred and ninety-nine of 'em go
By your looks, or your acts, or your glory.
But if he finds you and you find him,
The rest of the world don't matter;
For the Thousandth Man will sink or swim
With you in any water.

You can use his purse with no more talk
Than he uses yours for his spendings,
And laugh and meet in your daily walk
As though there had been no lendings.
Nine hundred and ninety-nine of them call
For silver and gold in their dealings;
But the Thousandth Man he's worth 'em all,
Because you can show him your feelings.

His wrong's your wrong, and his right's your right,
In season or out of season.
Stand up and back it in all men's sight –
With *that* for your only reason!
Nine hundred and ninety-nine can't bide
The shame or mocking or laughter,
But the Thousandth Man will stand by your side
To the gallows-foot – and after!

Rudyard Kipling

ENOUGH ALREADY

At work there are five words that I have come to dread, 'Can I have a word,' which is code for 'I have a boring, intractable problem which I would like to discuss with you for at least two hours.' The domestic version of this is the spouse/partner who uses the first person plural to apportion blame, as in 'We seem to have run out of dustbin bags,' which really means, 'You've forgotten to buy any because you are incompetent and have no idea how to run a house.' I include these poems for those moments when an AK-47 would come in handy had you not forgotten to renew your firearms licence.

There Are Too Many People

There are too many people on earth
insipid, unsalted, rabbity, endlessly hopping.
They nibble the face of the earth to a desert.

D. H. Lawrence

Epigrams

My Latin has left me,
which may be as well.
They were brute engineers
and their afterlife, hell.

Only one tag stays:
a bird with no wings.
'*In medias res*'
in the middle of things.

I am weighed down by parents,
made mad by my child.
The late sky is sleeting
the garden is wild.

I slump on a chair
in the last glow day brings.
In media res
in the muddle of things.

Alison Brackenbury

Keeping on Top of Things

I want to be alone. But I have to see
the chiropodist, the dentist,
the car mechanic, the ear-syringer,
the roofer, the window cleaner,
and a man to cut back the creeper
which is forcing its way in
through the bedroom window.

Thank goodness I don't have to see
the manicurist, the otologist,
the arboriculturalist,
the reflexologist, the phrenologist
the hypnotherapist, the gynaecologist
the Chinese herbalist, or the psychiatrist –

at least not this week.

Connie Bensley

HOW TO BE A PERFECT PARENT

I wish it were that easy. One minute the experts tell you to listen to your baby and to follow her cues, and the next they are advocating controlled crying and tough love. There are no short cuts to bringing up children but I think these poems offer the kind of advice that doesn't go out of fashion.

Nettles

My son aged three fell in the nettle bed.
'Bed' seemed a curious name for those green spears
That regiment of spite behind the shed:
It was no place for rest. With sobs and tears
The boy came seeking comfort and I saw
White blisters beaded on his tender skin.
We soothed him till his pain was not so raw.
At last he offered us a watery grin,
And then I took my hook and honed the blade
And went outside and slashed in fury with it
Till not a nettle in that fierce parade
Stood upright anymore. Next task: I lit
A funeral pyre to burn the fallen dead.
But in two weeks the busy sun and rain
Had called up tall recruits behind the shed:
My son would often feel sharp wounds again.

Vernon Scannell

A Wish for My Children

On this doorstep I stand
year after year
to watch you going

and think: May you not
skin your knees. May you
not catch your fingers
in car doors. May
your hearts not break.

May tide and weather
wait for your coming

and may you grow strong
to break
all webs of my weaving.

Evangeline Paterson

First Lesson

The thing to remember about fathers is, they're men.
A girl has to keep it in mind.
They are dragon-seekers, bent on improbable rescues.
Scratch any father, you find
Someone chock-full of qualms and romantic terrors,
Believing change is a threat –
Like your first shoes with heels on, like your first bicycle
It took such months to get.

Walk in strange woods, they warn you about the snakes
       there.
Climb, and they fear you'll fall.
Books, angular toys, or swimming in deep water –
Fathers mistrust them all.
Men are the worriers. It is difficult for them
To learn what they must learn:
How you have a journey to take and very likely,
For a while, will not return.

Phyllis McGinley

L PLATES

I make no apology for including a love section in a book about keeping your sanity. Falling in love is clearly a form of madness, as these poems show. But who wants to be sane all the time?

This Morning

This morning I will not
Comb my hair.
It has lain
Pillowed on the hand of my lover.

Hitomaro

Es Stehen Unbeweglich

The stars, for many ages,
Have dwelt in heaven above;
They gaze at one another
Tormented by their love.

They speak the richest language,
The loveliest ever heard;
Yet none of all the linguists
Can understand a word.

I learned it, though, in lessons
That nothing can erase;
The only text I needed
Was my beloved's face.

Heinrich Heine
translated by Aaron Kramer

Nothing

I take a jewel from a junk-shop tray
And wish I had a love to buy it for.
Nothing I choose will make you turn my way.
Nothing I give will make you love me more.

I know that I've embarrassed you too long
And I'm ashamed to linger at your door.
Whatever I embark on will be wrong.
Nothing I do will make you love me more.

I cannot work. I cannot read or write.
How can I frame a letter to implore.
Eloquence is a lie. The truth is trite.
Nothing I say will make you love me more.

So I replace the jewel in the tray
And laughingly pretend I'm far too poor.
Nothing I give, nothing I do or say,
Nothing I am will make you love me more.

James Fenton

Love Without Hope

Love without hope, as when the young bird-catcher
Swept off his tall hat to the Squire's own daughter,
So let the imprisoned larks escape and fly
Singing about her head, as she rode by.

Robert Graves

TIME TO GROW UP

You spend your teenage years desperate to grow up, you just can't wait to get away from the horrors of home. But then in your twenties home begins to look rather attractive, all the comforts of a hotel without the bills. Grown up sounds glamorous when it means driving round town in your parents' car, but not when it means grappling with bank statements. I think the Australian poet Myron Lysenko has written the manifesto for the reluctant grown up in his poem 'Pets and Death and Indoor Plants', and the Paul Summers poem should be uncomfortable reading for any twenty or even thirty something still living at their mum's and watching daytime TV.

Pets and Death and Indoor Plants

We're becoming old enough
to want to change our life-styles;
we're looking for substitutes
for sex & drugs and rock & roll.

But our dog . . . died
our cat . . . collapsed
budgies . . . wouldn't . . . budge.
Our roses . . . sank
our ferns . . . fizzled
cactus . . . carked it.

Yet, seated around roast dinners
our parents still talk about
the possibility of grandchildren.

Our minds . . . boggle
our bodies . . . fidget
our voices . . . falter.

We're still immature
& we'd like to be
for a few years yet.

The world's not ready for our baby;
we're not ready for the world.
We're still trying to learn

how to make love properly;
still trying to come to terms
with pets & death & indoor plants.

Myron Lysenko

D'ya Ever Have One of Those Days Tommy?

When even sticking on
the telly for lunchtime
neighbours is a bit of an
           effort?

When you guzzle
         milk
instead of tea 'cos
you can't be arsed
to wait for the
        kettle?

d'y'ever just sit
in an armchair for a whole
afternoon and think
how it felt to be cast in
         ironside?

Or count up the
      speckles on a
woodchipped wall?

sometimes after
casualty I think I've got
          cancer,
I think that I'm dying,
when really I'm just
       bored.

Paul Summers

WANTING A CHILD

I suppose one manifestation of growing up is the moment when you stop
worrying that you might be pregnant and instead you start worrying that
you might not be, or if you are a man that you are shooting blanks.
Nothing is more frustrating than 'letting nature take its course' and finding
that her master plan is for you to be everyone's favourite aunt or uncle.
'Just relax,' say well meaning friends, 'It'll happen if you don't think about
it.' But as anyone with fertility problems knows, relaxing when each
month might be *the* month is hardly possible. Read these poems and know
that however angry and desperate you are feeling, you are not alone.

Childless

Strong biceps
Firm thighs,
Big bottom
Sexy eyes,
Fast
On the track,
Strong like
A lion,
Good Kung-fu feet
And healthy hair.

Strong triceps
No lie,
Rhymster
Nice guy,

A good healthy back
Great levels of iron,
There must be a baby
In there
Somewhere,
There must be
A baby
In here.

Benjamin Zephaniah

Antarctica

I do not know what other women know.
I covet their children; wardrobes
stocked with blue or pink, froth-lace
bootees for the animal-child
that bleeds them.

Their calmness settles like the
ebb-tide on island shores –
nursing pearl-conch, secret fronds
of wisdom, certitude.
Their bellies taunt.

I do not know what other women know.
Breasts await the animal-child.
I want – maddened by
lunar crumblings, the false prophecy
of tingling breasts, turgid abdomen.

Antarctica: The storm petrel hovers;
waters petrified by spittled winds:
Little fish will not swim here.
Folds of bed-sheet take my face.
Blood seeps, again.

'But you are free', they cry,
'You have no child!' – bitterness
from women grafted like young willows,
forced before time. In Antarctica,
who will share this freedom?

Mary O'Donnell

DO THE RIGHT THING

In this section I have looked for words to live life by. I like the Maya Angelou poem for its muscular defiance of failure, but I also admire Marianne Moore's poem about the virtues of restraint. I just wish I could translate their words into my actions.

Man is Dear to Man

Man is dear to man: the poorest poor
Long for some moments in a weary life
When they can know and feel that they have been
Themselves the fathers and the givers-out
Of some small blessings; have been kind to such
As needed kindness, for the single cause
That we have all of us one common heart.

William Wordsworth

If I Can Stop One Heart from Breaking

If I can stop one heart from breaking,
   I shall not live in vain;
If I can ease one life the aching,
   Or cool one pain,
Or help one lonely person
   Into happiness again
I shall not live in vain.

Emily Dickinson

Ships?

Ships?
Sure I'll sail them.
Show me the boat,
If it'll float,
I'll sail it.

Men?
Yes I'll love them.
If they've got the style,
To make me smile,
I'll love them.

Life?
'Course I'll live it.
Let me have breath,
Just to my death,
And I'll live it.

Failure?
I'm not ashamed to tell it,
I never learned to spell it.
Not Failure.

Maya Angelou

Happy the Man

Happy the man, and happy he alone,
   He who can call today his own:
   He who, secure within, can say,
Tomorrow do thy worst, for I have lived today.
   Be fair or foul or rain or shine
The joys I have possessed, in spite of fate, are mine.
Not Heaven itself upon the past has power,
But what has been, has been, and I have had my hour.

John Dryden
translation of Horace, *Odes*, Book III, xxix

Silence

My father used to say,
'Superior people never make long visits,
have to be shown Longfellow's grave
or the glass flowers at Harvard.
Self-reliant like the cat—
that takes its prey to privacy,
the mouse's limp tail hanging like a shoelace from its
        mouth—
they sometimes enjoy solitude,
and can be robbed of speech
by speech which has delighted them.
The deepest feeling always shows itself in silence;
not in silence, but restraint'.
Nor was he insincere in saying, 'Make my house your inn'.
Inns are not residences.

Marianne Moore

OTHER PEOPLE'S MONEY

The really taboo question is not 'How often do you have sex?' but 'How much do you earn?' Other people's bank accounts, like their relationships, are mysterious and always seem much fuller than your own. But unless all your friends have trust funds you can be sure that they too are looking at you and wildly overestimating your net worth. These poems are to reassure you that while the rich are different, they don't necessarily have more fun. The only advantage of money is as F. Scott Fitzgerald points out at the end of *The Great Gatsby*, it gives you something to retreat into. But read the Do The Right Thing section and you won't need to run away.

Money

Quarterly, is it, money reproaches me:
    'Why do you let me lie here wastefully?
I am all you never had of goods and sex.
    You could get them still by writing a few cheques.'

So I look at others, what they do with theirs:
    They certainly don't keep it upstairs.
By now they've a second house and car and wife:
    Clearly money has something to do with life

– In fact, they've a lot in common, if you enquire:
    You can't put off being young until you retire,
And however you bank your screw, the money you save
    Won't in the end buy you more than a shave.

I listen to money singing. It's like looking down
　　From long french windows at a provincial town,
The slums, the canal, the churches ornate and mad
　　In the evening sun. It is intensely sad.

Philip Larkin

The Hardship of Accounting

Never ask of money spent
Where the spender thinks it went.
Nobody was ever meant
To remember or invent
What he did with every cent.

Robert Frost

Money

I was led into captivity by the bitch business
Not in love but in what seemed a physical necessity
And now I cannot even watch the spring
The itch for subsistence having become responsibility.

Money the she-devil comes to us under many veils
Tactful at first, calling herself beauty
Tear away this disguise, she proposes paternal solicitude
Assuming the dishonest face of duty.

Suddenly you are in bed with a screeching tear-sheet
This is money at last without her night-dress
Clutching you against her fallen udders and sharp bones
In an unscrupulous and deserved embrace.

C. H. Sisson

UNHOLY MATRIMONY

These are poems for those days when you just want to get in the car and keep on driving, or better still get in the car and reverse over your spouse. But if you can't face the mess and the possible damage to your tyres, then read these poems before consulting your lawyer. Who knows, after reading the Marge Piercy poem you may decide that your particular frog isn't so bad after all. I apologise to male readers for the rather hostile tone of this section, I did look for disillusioned husband poems but without success – male poets must have exceptional wives. The most cynical poem about marriage I have found is by Philip Larkin, who never married: My wife and I – we're *pals*. Marriage is *fun*. / Yes: two can live as stupidly as one.

Buttons

Perhaps you don't love me at all,
but at least you sew buttons on my coat
which is more than my wife does.

Adrian Henri

Mrs Icarus

I'm not the first or the last
to stand on a hillock,
watching the man she married
prove to the world
he's a total, utter, absolute, Grade A pillock.

Carol Ann Duffy

A Story Wet as Tears

Remember the princess who kissed the frog
so he became a prince? At first they danced
all weekend, toasted each other in the morning
with coffee, with champagne at night
and always with kisses. Perhaps it was
in bed after the first year had ground
around she noticed he had become cold
with her. She had to sleep
with heating pad and down comforter.
His manner grew increasingly chilly
and damp when she entered a room.
He spent his time in water sports,
hydroponics, working on his insect
collection.

          Then in the third year
when she said to him one day, my dearest,
are you taking your vitamins daily,
you look quite green, he leaped
away from her.

                Finally on their
fifth anniversary she confronted him.
'My precious, don't you love me any
more?' He replied, 'Rivet. Rivet.'
Though courtship turns frogs into princes,
marriage turns them quietly back.

Marge Piercy

Man in Space

All you have to do is listen to the way a man
sometimes talks to his wife at a table of people
and notice how intent he is on making his point
even though her lower lip is beginning to quiver,

and you will know why the women in science
fiction movies who inhabit a planet of their own
are not pictured making a salad or reading a magazine
when the men from earth arrive in their rocket,

why they are always standing in a semicircle
with their arms folded, their bare legs set apart,
their breasts protected by hard metal disks.

Billy Collins

WHY ARE THEY LOOKING AT ME LIKE THAT?

The membrane between madness and sanity is more delicate than it is safe to imagine. After a week of severely interrupted nights I became convinced that my baby's rocking swing was talking to me. It was a benign, though repetitive, conversationalist. 'Have a nice day' it said over and over. I decided to go to bed before I started seeing the face of Elvis in my daughter's baby rice. The first two poems are for those days when you are beginning to wonder whether you come from a different planet: I think everyone should learn the Emily Dickinson poem by heart, it is extremely useful in almost all circumstances. The Dorothy Nimmo poem is a reminder that modern life breeds its own madness.

Much Madness is Divinest Sense

Much Madness is divinest Sense
To a discerning Eye—
Much Sense – the starkest Madness –
'Tis the Majority
In this, as All, prevail –
Assent – and you are sane
Demur – you're straightway dangerous—
And handled with a Chain –

Emily Dickinson

Counting the Mad

This one was put in a jacket,
This one was sent home,
This one was given bread and meat
But would eat none,
And this one cried No No No No
All day long.

This one looked at the window
As though it were a wall,
This one saw things that were not there,
This one things that were,
And this one cried No No No No
All day long.

This one thought himself a bird,
This one a dog,
And this one thought himself a man,
An ordinary man,
And cried and cried No No No No
All day long.

Donald Justice

Who's Afraid

I don't eat meat, I'm afraid.
I don't eat any dairy products,
or sugar, salt, or artificial sweeteners.
It's inconvenient but I'm afraid
I don't eat processed food of any kind
because of the additives. I don't smoke
I don't drink coffee, tea or alcohol,
I drink only purified bottled water.
I don't take drugs, even on prescription.

Stay out of the rain, it is killing the forests.
Stay out of the sun, the ozone layer is thinning.
Stay out of the sea, it is thick with oil and sewage.
Stay out of the air, it is heavy with heavy metals.

Sterilize the drinking vessels
the eating vessels the knives and forks
and all the working surfaces. Everything
must be sterile.

I am no longer sexually active.

Seal the door and windows.
Keep a light burning day and night.

Dorothy Nimmo

BE HERE NOW

People who meditate on a daily basis are not only smug but annoyingly unlined. I find emptying my mind impossible in a world of small children, dogs and mobile telephones. But poems like the ones here are like tiny doors opening into a world of serenity. Read them slowly, savour their meaning and let your worries subside. As Wordsworth put it two hundred odd years ago, 'The world is too much with us: late and soon/ Getting and spending, we lay waste our powers.'

Out There

Do they ever meet out there,
The dolphins I counted,
The otter I wait for?
I should have spent my life
Listening to the waves.

Michael Longley

The world is too much with us: late and soon.
Getting and spending, we lay waste our powers:
Little we see in nature that is ours;
We have given our hearts away, a sordid boon!
This Sea that bares her bosom to the moon;
The Winds that will be howling at all hours
And are up-gathered now like sleeping flowers;
For this, for every thing, we are out of tune;
It moves us not. Great God! I'd rather be
A Pagan suckled in a creed outworn;
So might I, standing on this pleasant lea,
Have glimpses that would make me less forlorn;
Have sight of Proteus coming from the sea;
Or hear old Triton blow his wreathèd horn.

William Wordsworth

Voices

Voices in my head,
Chanting, 'Kisses. Bread.
Prove yourself. Fight. Shove.
Learn. Earn. Look for love,'

Drown a lesser voice,
Silent now of choice:
'Breathe in peace, and be
Still, for once, like me.'

Vikram Seth

I Meant to Do My Work Today

I meant to do my work today –
But a brown bird sang in the apple tree,
And a butterfly flitted across the field,
And all the leaves were calling me.

And the wind went sighing over the land
Tossing the grasses to and fro,
And a rainbow held out its shining hand –
So what could I do but laugh and go?

Richard LeGallienne

in time's a noble mercy of proportion
with generosities beyond believing
(though flesh and blood accuse him of coercion
or mind and soul convict him of deceiving)

whose ways are neither reasoned nor unreasoned,
his wisdom cancels conflict and agreement
—saharas have their centuries;ten thousand
of which are smaller than a rose's moment

there's time for laughing and there's time for crying—
for hoping for despair for peace for longing
—a time for growing and a time for dying:
a night for silence and a day for singing

but more than all(as all your more than eyes
tell me)there is a time for timelessness

E. E. Cummings

GETTING OVER IT

Poets must be the only people in the world who can profit from a broken heart. The emotional turmoil is tiresome at the time, of course, but it is all useful material. There are poems here for every stage of the road to recovery. The poems by Hugo Williams and Lorna Goodison are a reminder not to get stuck in the self pity groove. The poems by Pushkin and the Edwardian poet Charlotte Mew invoke the desired note of poignant acceptance. My own favourite is by the Russian poet Vladimir Mayakovsky. Perhaps I shouldn't reveal that this poem was found in Mayakovsky's pocket after he shot himself, but then poets don't have to be consistent. Unlike Mayakovsky you will get over it.

Tonight I Can Write

Tonight I can write the saddest lines.

Write, for example, 'The night is shattered
and the blue stars shiver in the distance.'

The night wind revolves in the sky and sings.

Tonight, I can write the saddest lines.
I loved her, and sometimes she loved me too.

Through nights like this one, I held her in my arms.
I kissed her again and again under the endless sky.

She loved me, sometimes I loved her too.
How could one not have loved her great still eyes.

Tonight I can write the saddest lines.
To think that I do not have her. To feel that I have lost her.

To hear the immense night, still more immense without her.
And the verse falls to the soul like dew to the pasture.

What does it matter that my love could not keep her.
The night is shattered and she is not with me.

This is all. In the distance someone is singing. In the
      distance.
My soul is not satisfied that it has lost her.

My sight searches for her as though to go to her.
My heart looks for her, and she is not with me.

The same night whitening the same trees.
We, of that time, are no longer the same.

I no longer love her, that's certain, but how I loved her.
My voice tried to find the wind to touch her hearing.

Another's. She will be another's. Like my kisses before.
Her voice. Her bright body. Her infinite eyes.

I no longer love her, that's certain, but maybe I love her.
Love is so short, forgetting is so long.

Because through nights like this one I held her in my arms
my soul is not satisfied that it has lost her.

Though this be the last pain that she makes me suffer
and these the last verses that I write for her.

Pablo Neruda

Everyone Knows This

How am I feeling this morning?
Or is it too early to say?
I check by swallowing
to see if my throat's still sore.
I check by thinking
to see if my brain still hurts.

I'm walking along out of doors,
not feeling anything much,
when it suddenly comes to me:
I don't feel so bad any more.
I think to myself,
'I'll soon put a stop to that!'

Hugo Williams

Of Bitterness Herbs

You knotted the spite blooms into a bouquet-garni
to flavor stock for sour soups and confusion stews.
Now no one will dine with you.

A diet of bitterness is self consuming. Such herbs
are best destroyed, rooted out from the garden
of the necessary even preordained past.

Bitter herbs grow luxuriant where the grudgeful crow
dropped its shadow, starting a compost heap of need in you
to spray malicious toxins over all flowers in our rose
        gardens.

Bitterness herbs bake bad-minded bread, are good for little
except pickling green-eyed gall stones, then eaten alone
from wooden spoons of must-suck-salt.

Lorna Goodison

I Loved You

I loved you; even now I may confess,
   Some embers of my love their fire retain;
But do not let it cause you more distress,
   I do not want to sadden you again.
Hopeless and tonguetied, yet I loved you dearly
   With pangs the jealous and the timid know,
So tenderly I loved you, so sincerely,
   I pray God grant another love you so.

Alexander Pushkin
translated by Reginald Mainwaring Hewitt

I So Liked Spring

I so liked Spring last year
        Because you were here; –
              The thrushes too –
Because it was these you so liked to hear –
            I so liked you.

    This year's a different thing, –
             I'll not think of you.
But I'll like Spring because it is simply Spring
          As the thrushes do.

Charlotte Mew

Past One O'Clock . . .

Past one o'clock. You must have gone to bed.
The Milky Way streams silver through the night.
I'm in no hurry; with lightning telegrams
I have no cause to wake or trouble you.
And, as they say, the incident is closed.
Love's boat has smashed against the daily grind.
Now you and I are quits. Why bother then
To balance mutual sorrows, pains, and hurts.
Behold what quiet settles on the world.
Night wraps the sky in tribute from the stars.
In hours like these, one rises to address
The ages, history, and all creation.

Vladimir Mayakovsky

SAYING GOODBYE

I have included here poems for moments of private mourning – the Tony Harrison poem for example – and others such as the famous passage from Shakespeare's *Cymbeline* or the W. E. Henley poem which could be read aloud at a funeral. R. S. Thomas's poem 'A Marriage' manages to make grief, the clumsiest of emotions, somehow graceful.

Remember

Remember me when I am gone away,
   Gone far away into the silent land;
   When you can no more hold me by the hand,
Nor I half turn to go yet turning stay.
Remember me when no more day by day
   You tell me of our future that you planned:
   Only remember me; you understand
It will be late to counsel then or pray.
Yet if you should forget me for a while
   And afterwards remember, do not grieve:
   For if the darkness and corruption leave
   A vestige of the thoughts that once I had,
Better by far you should forget and smile
   Than that you should remember and be sad.

Christina G. Rossetti

Going Without Saying

(In memory of Joe Flynn)

It is a great pity we don't know
When the dead are going to die
So that, over a last companionable
Drink, we could tell them
How much we liked them.

Happy the man who, dying, can
Place his hand on his heart and say:
'At least I didn't neglect to tell
The thrush how beautifully she sings.'

Bernard O'Donoghue

Though my mother was already two years dead
Dad kept her slippers warming by the gas,
put hot water bottles her side of the bed
and still went to renew her transport pass.

You couldn't just drop in. You had to phone.
He'd put you off an hour to give him time
to clear away her things and look alone
as though his still raw love were such a crime.

He couldn't risk my blight of disbelief
though sure that very soon he'd hear her key
scrape in the rusted lock and end his grief.
He *knew* she'd just popped out to get the tea.

I believe life ends with death, and that is all.
You haven't both gone shopping; just the same,
in my new black leather phone book there's your name
and the disconnected number I still call.

Tony Harrison
from 'Long Distance'

So Be My Passing

A late lark twitters from the quiet skies
And from the west,
Where the sun, his day's work ended,
Lingers as in content,
There falls on the old, gray city
An influence luminous and serene,
A shining peace.

The smoke ascends
In a rosy-and-golden haze. The spires
Shine and are changed. In the valley
Shadows rise. The lark sings on. The sun,
Closing his benediction,
Sinks, and the darkening air
Thrills with a sense of the triumphing night –
Night with her train of stars
And her great gift of sleep.

So be my passing!
My task accomplish'd and the long day done,
My wages taken, and in my heart
Some late lark singing,
Let me be gather'd to the quiet west,
The sundown splendid and serene,
Death.

W. E. Henley

Fear No More

Fear no more the heat o' th' sun
Nor the furious winter's rages;
Thou thy worldly task hast done,
Home art gone, and ta'en thy wages.
Golden lads and girls all must,
As chimney sweepers, come to dust.

Fear no more the frown o' th' great;
Thou art past the tyrant's stroke.
Care no more to clothe and eat;
To thee the reed is as the oak.
The sceptre, learning physic, must
All follow this and come to dust.

Fear no more the lightning flash,
Nor th' all-dreaded thunder-stone;
Fear not slander, censure rash;
Thou hast finish'd joy and moan.
All lovers young, all lovers must
Consign to thee and come to dust.

No exorciser harm thee!
Nor no witchcraft charm thee!
Ghost unlaid forbear thee!
Quiet consummation have,
And renowned by thy grave!

William Shakespeare
from *Cymbeline*, Act IV, Scene ii

A Marriage

We met
        under a shower
of bird-notes.
        Fifty years passed,
love's moment
        in a world in
servitude to time.
        She was young;
I kissed with my eyes
        closed and opened
them on her wrinkles.
        'Come,' said death,
choosing her as his
        partner for
the last dance. And she,
        who in life
had done everything
        with a bird's grace,
opened her bill now
        for the shedding
of one sigh no
        heavier than a feather.

R. S. Thomas

BLACK HOLE

None of these poems is exactly cheering, if you want hope turn to the next section. But when you are at the bottom of the black hole with no handholds visible, what you want is not optimism but some reassurance that you are not alone. There is every gradation of gloom here; from Auden's unflinching 'Musée des Beaux Arts', to the terminal bleakness of Philip Larkin's 'Wants'. The only way out is to look calmly at what Robert Frost calls 'your own desert places'.

Advice from the Experts

I lay down in the empty street and parked
My feet against the gutter's curb while from
The building above a bunch of gawkers perched
Along its ledges urged me don't, don't jump.

Bill Knott

Musée des Beaux Arts

About suffering they were never wrong,
The Old Masters: how well they understood
Its human position; how it takes place
While someone else is eating or opening a window or just
     walking dully along;
How, when the aged are reverently, passionately waiting
For the miraculous birth, there always must be
Children who did not specially want it to happen, skating
On a pond at the edge of the wood:
They never forgot
That even the dreadful martyrdom must run its course
Anyhow in a corner, some untidy spot
Where the dogs go on with their doggy life and the
     torturer's horse
Scratches its innocent behind on a tree.

In Brueghel's *Icarus*, for instance: how everything turns
     away
Quite leisurely from the disaster; the ploughman may
Have heard the splash, the forsaken cry,
But for him it was not an important failure; the sun shone
As it had to on the white legs disappearing into the green
Water; and the expensive delicate ship that must have seen
Something amazing, a boy falling out of the sky,
Had somewhere to get to and sailed calmly on.

W. H. Auden

Wants

Beyond all this, the wish to be alone:
However the sky grows dark with invitation-cards
However we follow the printed directions of sex
However the family is photographed under the flagstaff –
Beyond all this, the wish to be alone.

Beneath it all, desire of oblivion runs:
Despite the artful tensions of the calendar,
The life insurance, the tabled fertility rites,
The costly aversion of the eyes from death –
Beneath it all, desire of oblivion runs.

Philip Larkin

Desert Places

Snow falling and night falling fast, oh, fast
In a field I looked into going past,
And the ground almost covered smooth in snow,
But a few weeds and stubble showing last.

The woods around it have it – it is theirs.
All animals are smothered in their lairs.
I am too absent-spirited to count;
The loneliness includes me unawares.

And lonely as it is that loneliness
Will be more lonely ere it will be less –
A blanker whiteness of benighted snow
With no expression, nothing to express.

They cannot scare me with their empty spaces
Between stars – on stars where no human race is.
I have it in me so much nearer home
To scare myself with my own desert places.

Robert Frost

EMOTIONAL RESCUE

Turn to this section when you've had your fill of despair and you'd like the sun to come out again. I love Emily Dickinson's poem that begins '"Hope" is the thing with feathers/ That perches in the soul.' And Sydney Smith's advice to the low spirited, although not a poem, is so sensible (except his suggestion to avoid poetry) that I had to include it.

El Hombre

It's a strange courage
you give me ancient star:

Shine alone in the sunrise
toward which you lend no part!

William Carlos Williams

Celia, Celia

When I am sad and weary
When I think all hope is gone
When I walk along High Holborn
I think of you with nothing on

Adrian Mitchell

'Hope' is the Thing with Feathers

'Hope' is the thing with feathers –
That perches in the soul –
And sings the tune without the words –
And never stops – at all –

And sweetest – in the Gale – is heard –
And sore must be the storm –
That could abash the little Bird
That kept so many warm –

I've heard it in the chillest land –
And on the strangest Sea –
Yet, never, in Extremity,
It asked a crumb – of Me.

Emily Dickinson

Advice on Low Spirits

Nobody has suffered more from low spirits than I have done, so I feel for you.

1. Live as well and drink as much wine as you dare. 2. Go in to the shower-bath with a small quantity of water at a temperature low enough to give you a *slight* sensation of cold – 75 or 80°. 3. Amusing books. 4. Short views of human life not farther than dinner or tea. 5. Be as busy as you can. 6. See as much as you can of those friends who respect and like you; 7. and of those acquaintances who amuse you. 8. Make no secret of low spirits to your friends but talk of them fully: they are always the worse for dignified concealment. 9. Attend to the effects tea and coffee produce upon you. 10. Compare your lot with that of other people. 11. Don't expect too much of human life, a sorry business at best. 12. Avoid poetry, dramatic representations (except comedy), music, serious novels, melancholy sentimental people, and everything likely to excite feeling or emotion not ending in active benevolence. 13. Do good and endeavour to please everybody of every degree. 14. Be as much as you can in the open air without fatigue. 15. Make the room where you commonly sit gay and pleasant. 15. Struggle little by little against idleness. 17. Don't be too severe upon yourself, but do yourself justice. 18. Keep good, blazing fires. 19. Be firm and constant in the exercise of rational religion. 20. Believe me dear Lady Georgiana very truly yours,

Sydney Smith

WHAT ARE YOU WAITING FOR?

The words here may share a sombre base line, but they each offer a
reminder that time is running out. You can either be terrified by this
thought or it can set you free. To quote Andrew Marvell in 'To His Coy
Mistress': 'The grave's a fine and private place/ But none I think, do there
embrace.' Get to it. There's no time to lose.

Candles

Days to come stand in front of us
like a row of burning candles –
golden, warm, and vivid candles.

Days past fall behind us,
a gloomy line of burnt-out candles;
the nearest are still smoking,
cold, melted, and bent.

I don't want to look at them: their shape saddens me,
and it saddens me to remember their original light.
I look ahead at my burning candles.

I don't want to turn, don't want to see, terrified,
how quickly that dark line gets longer,
how quickly one more dead candle joins another.

C. P. Cavafy

Memento Mori

There is no need for me to keep a skull on my desk,
to stand with one foot up on the ruins of Rome,
or wear a locket with the sliver of a saint's bone.

It is enough to realize that every common object
in this sunny little room will outlive me –
the carpet, radio, bookstand and rocker.

Not one of these things will attend my burial,
not even this dented goosenecked lamp
with its steady benediction of light,

though I could put worse things in my mind
than the image of it waddling across the cemetery
like an old servant, dragging the tail of its cord,
the small circle of mourners parting to make room.

Billy Collins

Madam Life's a piece in bloom

Madam Life's a piece in bloom
   Death goes dogging everywhere:
She's the tenant of the room,
   He's the ruffian on the stair.

You shall see her as a friend,
   You shall bilk him once or twice;
But he'll trap you in the end,
   And he'll stick you for her price.

With his kneebones at your chest,
   And his knuckles in your throat,
You would reason – plead – protest!
   Clutching at her petticoat;

But she's heard it all before,
   Well she knows you've had your fun,
Gingerly she gains the door,
   And your little job is done.

W. E. Henley

Leap Before You Look

The sense of danger must not disappear:
The way is certainly both short and steep,
However gradual it looks from here;
Look if you like, but you will have to leap.

Tough-minded men get mushy in their sleep
And break the by-laws any fool can keep;
It is not the convention but the fear
That has a tendency to disappear.

The worried efforts of the busy heap,
The dirt, the imprecision, and the beer
Produce a few smart wisecracks every year;
Laugh if you can, but you will have to leap.

The clothes that are considered right to wear
Will not be either sensible or cheap,
So long as we consent to live like sheep
And never mention those who disappear.

W. H. Auden

ACKNOWLEDGEMENTS

INDEX OF POETS

INDEX

ACKNOWLEDGEMENTS

We are grateful for permission to reprint the following copyright poems in this collection:

MAYA ANGELOU: 'On Reaching Forty', 'Ships?', 'The Health-Food Diner', and 'The Telephone' from *Complete Collected Poems* (Virago, 1994), reprinted by permission of the publishers, Little, Brown & Company (UK). W H AUDEN: 'Musée des Beaux Arts' and 'Leap Before You Look' from *Collected Poems* (1976), reprinted by permission of the publishers, Faber & Faber Ltd. ALAN AYCKBOURN: 'Here's an Announcement' from 'Seven Fragments', copyright © Haydonning Ltd 1986, first published in *Occasional Poets* edited by Richard Adams (Viking, 1986), reprinted by permission of Casarotto Ramsay Associates Ltd on behalf of the author. HILAIRE BELLOC: 'The Vulture' from *Complete Verse* (Pimlico/Random), reprinted by permission of PFD on behalf of the Estate of Hilaire Belloc. CONNIE BENSLEY: 'Insomnia', 'Keeping on Top of Things', and 'Twelve Things I Don't Want to Hear' from *The Back and the Front of It* (2000), reprinted by permission of the publisher, Bloodaxe Books. ALISON BRACKENBURY: 'Epigrams' first published in *Poetry Review* 89, No 4 (1999/2000), reprinted by permission of the author. NORMAN CAMERON: 'The Compassionate Fool' from *Collected Poems and Selected Translations* edited by Warren Hope and Jonathan Barker (1990), reprinted by permission of the publisher, Anvil Press Poetry. C P CAVAFY: 'Candles' from *Collected Poems* (Hogarth Press, 1990), reprinted by permission of the translators, Edmund Keeley and Philip Sherrard, the Estate of C P Cavafy, and the publishers, The Random House Group Ltd. ALISON CHISHOLM: 'Office Party' from *Daring the Slipstream* (Headland, 1997), first published in *And Somewhere a Sea ...* (Southport Writers Circle, 1991), reprinted by permission of the author. BILLY COLLINS: 'Man in Space' and 'Memento Mori' from *Taking Off Emily Dickinson's Clothes* (Picador Macmillan, 2000), copyright © Billy Collins 2000, reprinted by permission of Macmillan Publishers. WENDY COPE: 'Message' from *Making Cocoa for Kingsley Amis* (1986), 'The New Regime' from *Serious Concerns* (1992), and 'The Sorrow of Socks' from *If I Don't Know* (2001), reprinted by permission of the publishers, Faber & Faber Ltd. E E CUMMINGS: 'in time's a noble mercy of proportion' from *Complete Poems 1904-1962* edited by George J Firmage, copyright © 1991 by the Trustees for the E E Cummings Trust and George James Firmage, reprinted by permission of W W Norton & Company. DICK DAVIS: '6 a.m. Thoughts' from *Devices and Desires: New and Selected Poems 1967-1987* (1989), reprinted by permission of the publisher, Anvil Press Poetry. EMILY DICKINSON: poem #182 '"Hope" is the thing with feathers', poem #435 'Much madness is divinest sense' and poem #919 'If I can stop one heart from breaking' from *The Poems of Emily Dickinson*, edited by Thomas H Johnson, (The Belknap Press of Harvard University Press), copyright © 1951, 1955, 1979 by the President and Fellows of Harvard College, reprinted by permission of the publishers

Five' from *Small Arms Practice* (Wm Heinemann, Australia, 1989), reprinted by permission of Curtis Brown (Aust) Pty Ltd on behalf of the author. **VERNON SCANNELL**: 'Nettles' from *Mastering the Craft* (Pergamon, 1970), reprinted by permission of the author. **VIKRAM SETH**: 'Vices' from *All You Who Sleep Tonight* (Faber, 1990), copyright © Vikram Seth 1990, reprinted by permission of Sheil Land Associates Ltd. **C H SISSON**: 'Money' from *Collected Poems* (1998), reprinted by permission of the publishers, Carcanet Press Ltd. **STEVIE SMITH**: 'Lady "Rogue" Singleton' from *Collected Poems of Stevie Smith*, copyright © 1972 Stevie Smith, reprinted by permission of the Executors of James McGibbon. **PAUL SUMMERS**: 'D'Ya Ever Have One of Those Days, Tommy?' from *The Last Bus* (Iron Press, 1998), reprinted by permission of the publisher on behalf of the author. **R S THOMAS**: 'A Marriage' and 'Journeys' from *Mass for Hard Times* (1992), reprinted by permission of the publisher, Bloodaxe Books. **STEVE TURNER**: 'British Rail Regrets' from *Up To Date* (1983), reprinted by permission of the publishers , Hodder & Stoughton, Ltd. **ALICE WALKER**: 'Every Morning' from *Horses Make a Landscape Look More Beautiful* (The Women's Press, 1985), reprinted by permission of David Higham Associates. **HUGO WILLIAMS**: 'Everyone Knows This' from *Billy's Rain* (1999), reprinted by permission of the publishers, Faber & Faber Ltd. **WILLIAM CARLOS WILLIAMS**: 'El Hombre' from *Collected Poems* (2000), reprinted by permission of the publishers, Carcanet Press Ltd. **BENJAMIN ZEPHANIAH**: 'Childless' from *Propa Propa ganda* (1996), reprinted by permission of the publisher, Bloodaxe Books.

Although we have tried to trace and contact all copyright holders before publication, this has not been possible in every case. If notified the publisher will be pleased to make any necessary arrangements at the earliest opportunity.

INDEX OF POETS

ANGELOU, MAYA
On Reaching Forty 19
Ships? 85
The Health-Food Diner 40
The Telephone 53

AUDEN, W. H.
Leap Before You Look 128
Musée des Beaux Arts 118

AYCKBOURN, ALAN
Here's an announcement 22

BELLOC, HILAIRE
The Vulture 12

BENSLEY, CONNIE
Insomnia 44
Keeping on Top of Things 68
Twelve Things I Don't Want to Hear 16

BRACKENBURY, ALISON
Epigrams 67

BUNYAN, JOHN
Upon the Snail 8

CAMERON, NORMAN
The Compassionate Fool 34

CAVAFY, C. P.
Candles 125

CHISHOLM, ALISON
Office Party 32

COLLINS, BILLY
Man in Space 95
Memento Mori 126

COOLIDGE, SUSAN
New Every Morning 49

COPE, WENDY
Message 51
The New Regime 11
The Sorrow of Socks 17

CUMMINGS, E. E.
In time's a noble mercy of proportion 103

DAVIS, DICK
6 a.m. Thoughts 45

DICKINSON, EMILY
'Hope' is the Thing with Feathers 123
If I Can Stop One Heart from Breaking 84
Much Madness is Divinest Sense 96

DRYDEN, JOHN
Happy the Man 86

DUFFY, CAROL ANN
Mrs Icarus 93

EMERSON, SALLY
Back to Work 60

EWART, GAVIN
The Meeting 27

FEINSTEIN, ELAINE
Getting Older 20

FENTON, JAMES
Nothing 74
Let's Go Over It All Again 39

FORTUNE, CHARLOTTE
Pls, stop sendg msgs2ths 3

FRIED, ERICH
Lots of Things 50
FROST, ROBERT
Desert Places 120
Fire and Ice 57
The Hardship of Accounting 90
FULLER, REAY
Redundancy Pay 33
GOODISON, LORNA
Of Bitterness Herbs 107
GRAVES, ROBERT
Love Without Hope 75
HARRISON, TONY
Though my mother 113
HEINE, HEINRICH
Es Stehen Unbeweglich 73
HENLEY, W. E.
Madam Life's a piece in bloom 127
So Be My Passing 114
HENRI, ADRIAN
Buttons 92
HERRICK, ROBERT
Here we are all 43
HITOMARO
This Morning 72
HOOD, THOMAS
No! 36
JUSTICE, DONALD
Counting the Mad 97
KENNEDY, X. J.
To Someone Who Insisted I Look Up Someone 62
KIPLING, RUDYARD
The Thousandth Man 64
KNOTT, BILL
Advice from the Experts 117

LARKIN, PHILIP
Marriage 92
Money 88
Wants 119
LAWRENCE, D. H.
There Are Too Many People 66
Beautiful Old Age 21
LEGALLIENNE, RICHARD
I Meant to Do My Work Today 102
LONGLEY, MICHAEL
Out There 99
LYSENKO, MYRON
Pets and Death and Indoor Plants 76
MASEFIELD, JOHN
An Epilogue 46
MAYAKOVSKY, VLADIMIR
Past One O'Clock 110
McGINLEY, PHYLLIS
First Lesson 71
MERWIN, W. S.
The Highway 25
MEW, CHARLOTTE
I So Liked Spring 109
MITCHELL, ADRIAN
Screw It Yourself 7
Celia, Celia 122
MOORE, MARIANNE
Silence 87
MULDOON, PAUL
A Stone 35
NASH, OGDEN
Crossing the Border 18
NERUDA, PABLO
Tonight I Can Write 104
NICHOLS, GRACE
Give Yourself a Hug 48

NIMMO, DOROTHY
Who's Afraid 98
NOLAN, JAMES
Modern Times 5
NORMAL, HENRY
Ten Ways to End a Relationship 55
O'DONNELL, MARY
Antarctica 81
O'DONOGHUE, BERNARD
Going Without Saying 112
O'DRISCOLL, DENNIS
Then the time comes 30
PATERSON, EVANGELINE
A Wish for My Children 70
PIERCY, MARGE
A Snarl for Loose Friends 63
Folding Sheets 13
A Story Wet as Tears 94
PLATH, SYLVIA
Child 59
POTTS, TABITHA
All Tears 61
PUGH, SHEENAGH
Sometimes 47
PUSHKIN, ALEXANDER
I Loved You 108
RAYMOND, VICKI
The Sending of Five 37
ROSSETTI, CHRISTINA G.
Remember 111
SCANNELL, VERNON
Nettles 69
SETH, VIKRAM
Voices 101

SHAKESPEARE, WILLIAM
Fear No More 115
SISSON, C. H.
Money 91
SMITH, STEVIE
Lady 'Rogue' Singleton 54
SMITH, SYDNEY
Recipe for a Salad 42
Advice on Low Spirits 124
SNEVE, VIRGINIA DRIVING HAWK
Sun, Moon, Stars 58
SUMMERS, PAUL
D'ya Ever Have One of Those Days Tommy? 78
THOMAS, R. S.
A Marriage 116
Journeys 26
TURNER, STEVE
British Rail Regrets 23
VANDAL, NORMAN
Spellbound 4
WALKER, ALICE
Every Morning 9
WILLIAMS, HUGO
Everyone Knows This 106
WILLIAMS, WILLIAM CARLOS
El Hombre 121
WORDSWORTH, WILLIAM
Man is Dear to Man 83
The world is too much with us 100
ZEPHANIAH, BENJAMIN
Childless 79
ANON
On a Tired Housewife 15

INDEX

you have performed an illegal action

Pls, stop sendg msgs2ths, Charlotte Fortune 3

Spellbound, Norman Vandal 4

Modern Times, James Nolan 5

flatpack frenzy

Screw It Yourself, Adrian Mitchell 7

Upon the Snail, John Bunyan 8

too solid flesh

Every Morning, Alice Walker 9

The New Regime, Wendy Cope 11

The Vulture, Hilaire Belloc 12

domestic goddess anxiety

Folding Sheets, Marge Piercy 13

On a Tired Housewife, Anon 15

Twelve Things I Don't Want to Hear, Connie Bensley 16

The Sorrow of Socks, Wendy Cope 17

crow's-feet

Crossing the Border, Ogden Nash 18

On Reaching Forty, Maya Angelou 19

Getting Older, Elaine Feinstein 20

Beautiful Old Age, D. H. Lawrence 21

in transit

Here's an announcement, Alan Ayckbourn 22

British Rail Regrets, Steve Turner 23

The Highway, W. S. Merwin 25

Journeys, R. S. Thomas 26

you don't have to be mad to work here

The Meeting, Gavin Ewart 27

Then the time comes, Dennis O'Driscoll 30

Office Party, Alison Chisholm 32

downsized

Redundancy Pay, Reay Fuller 33

The Compassionate Fool, Norman Cameron 34

endless winter

A Stone, Paul Muldoon 35

No!, Thomas Hood 36

hexes for your ex

The Sending of Five, Vicki Raymond 37

Let's Go Over It All Again, James Fenton 39

low blood sugar
The Health-Food Diner, Maya Angelou 40
Recipe for a Salad, Sydney Smith 42

can't sleep
Here we are all, Robert Herrick 43
Insomnia, Connie Bensley 44
6 a.m. Thoughts, Dick Davis 45

mental massage
An Epilogue, John Masefield 46
Sometimes, Sheenagh Pugh 47
Give Yourself a Hug, Grace Nichols 48
New Every Morning, Susan Coolidge 49

only connect
Lots of Things, Erich Fried 50
Message, Wendy Cope 51
The Telephone, Maya Angelou 53

50 ways to leave your lover
Lady 'Rogue' Singleton, Stevie Smith 54
Ten Ways to End a Relationship, Henry Normal 55
Fire and Ice, Robert Frost 57

baby love
Sun, Moon, Stars, Virginia Driving Hawk Sneve 58

Child, Sylvia Plath 59
Back to Work, Sally Emerson 60
All Tears, Tabitha Potts 61

through thick and thin
To Someone Who Insisted I Look Up Someone, X. J. Kennedy 62
A Snarl for Loose Friends, Marge Piercy 63
The Thousandth Man, Rudyard Kipling 64

enough already
There Are Too Many People, D. H. Lawrence 66
Epigrams, Alison Brackenbury 67
Keeping on Top of Things, Connie Bensley 68

how to be a perfect parent
Nettles, Vernon Scannell 69
A Wish for My Children, Evangeline Paterson 70
First Lesson, Phyllis McGinley 71

L plates
This Morning, Hitomaro 72
Es Stehen Unbeweglich, Heinrich Heine 73
Nothing, James Fenton 74
Love Without Hope, Robert Graves 75

time to grow up
Pets and Death and Indoor Plants, Myron Lysenko 76

D'ya Ever Have One of Those Days Tommy?, Paul Summers 78

wanting a child
Childless, Benjamin Zephaniah 79
Antarctica, Mary O'Donnell 81

do the right thing
Man is Dear to Man, William Wordsworth 83
If I Can Stop One Heart from Breaking, Emily Dickinson 84
Ships?, Maya Angelou 85
Happy the Man, John Dryden 86
Silence, Marianne Moore 87

other people's money
Money, Philip Larkin 88
The Hardship of Accounting, Robert Frost 90
Money, C. H. Sisson 91

unholy matrimony
Marriage, Philip Larkin 92
Buttons, Adrian Henri 92
Mrs Icarus, Carol Ann Duffy 93
A Story Wet as Tears, Marge Piercy 94
Man in Space, Billy Collins 95

why are they looking at me like that?
Much Madness is Divinest Sense, Emily Dickinson 96
Counting the Mad, Donald Justice 97

Who's Afraid, Dorothy Nimmo 98

be here now
Out There, Michael Longley 99
The world is too much with us, William Wordsworth 100
Voices, Vikram Seth 101
I Meant to Do My Work Today, Richard LeGallienne 102
in time's a noble mercy of proportion, E. E. Cummings 103

getting over it
Tonight I Can Write, Pablo Neruda 104
Everyone Knows This, Hugo Williams 106
Of Bitterness Herbs, Lorna Goodison 107
I Loved You, Alexander Pushkin 108
I So Liked Spring, Charlotte Mew 109
Past One O'Clock, Vladimir Mayakovsky 110

saying goodbye
Remember, Christina G. Rossetti 111
Going Without Saying, Bernard O'Donoghue 112
Though my mother, Tony Harrison 113
So Be My Passing, W. E. Henley 114

Fear No More, William
  Shakespeare 115
A Marriage, R. S. Thomas 116

black hole
Advice from the Experts, Bill Knott
  117
Musée des Beaux Arts, W. H.
  Auden 118
Wants, Philip Larkin 119
Desert Places, Robert Frost 120

emotional rescue
El Hombre, William Carlos
  Williams 121

Celia, Celia, Adrian Mitchell
  122
'Hope' is the Thing with Feathers,
  Emily Dickinson 123
Advice on Low Spirits, Sydney
  Smith 124

what are you waiting for?
Candles, C. P. Cavafy 125
Memento Mori, Billy Collins
  126
Madam Life's a piece in bloom,
  W. E. Henley 127
Leap Before You look, W. H. Auden
  128